Arthur Stringer

Watchers of Twilight

And Other Poems

Arthur Stringer

Watchers of Twilight
And Other Poems

ISBN/EAN: 9783337005856

Printed in Europe, USA, Canada, Australia, Japan

Cover: Foto ©Thomas Meinert / pixelio.de

More available books at **www.hansebooks.com**

WATCHERS ᴀ OF ᴀ TWILIGHT;

AND OTHER POEMS.

BY ARTHUR J. STRINGER . . .

LONDON, ONT.

T. H. WARREN, PRINTER.   1894.

CONTENTS.

— —

A Prelude.

What bird that wings the summer dawn
But half forgot its earthly home?
What bird when all the day is gone
But leaves the air its wild wings roam

And flutters through the twilight-grey,
Once more towards its earthly nest,
Not quite forgot through all the day,
And wide for that one wanderer's breast?

And I, who wandered far from thee,
'Neath northern star and southern sky
In fruitless tasks of minstrelsy,
Back to thine open heart shall fly ;

And in life's twilight homeward come,
And at the home-door we shall meet ;
And should my faltering lips be dumb,
I lay these gleanings at thy feet.

WATCHERS OF TWILIGHT.

Nec deus intersit, nisi dignus vindice nodus.

There was a time when sea and air and earth
Were filled with many voices of the gods;
And in all things there dwelt a deity.
The air once felt the silent flutterings
Of wandering angels on their azurn ways;
The sea-winds inland bore some wafted song
A white-armed goddess sang far overseas;
And woodland places heard the pipe of Pan.
'Twas in the dreaming childhood of the world,
The pale grey twilight of tellurian times,
When every vale was filled with shadowy sounds,
And all created things were dimly touched
With dawn's still dim and lingering light.
But o'er the ageing earth a change has crept.
Those old uncertain shades have passed away,
And we among our days' less golden lights
Look back on those twilight illusions old,
Half with regret and half with wonderment,
And feel the sorrow of a vanished dream,
The want of something strangely lost and gone;
The want that Summer feels when flower and song
Have wandered southward with the sleeping sun,
And she to Autumn's sober face doth turn
With silence, to her loss unreconciled.

* * * * *

No longer the Olympian Muses nine

Touch with celestial fire the suppliant's lip;
Aonian lights can never more illume
The darkling glooms of lingering poesy;
For now all songs grow sad or diffident,
And pensively our poets backward gaze,
And on the dead past, where their love still clings,
They press Niobean kisses tenderly;
Sad mothers— seeing not the tristful child
Who weeps with many a want beside her knee,
In clasping to her breast her infant dead.
No longer of ethereal asphodel
Or alien amaranth may they dream songs,
But of mere worldly roses lush with dew.
The olden unillumined lands of hope
Have grown ungoldened to our noonday eyes,
And even where those lands were wont to lie
There only dwells a wide grey watery waste,
A strange sad sea, where silence erewhile slept,
Unkeeled, untravelled, isling golden realms;
Not of a heaven brought to earth, but earth
Exalted by our thought's divinity.
For this the doctrine, ancient, deep, yet new,
All heavens are the rainbows born of pain;
Free earth from pain, and then the old ideal
And useless anodyne earth casts aside.
No exiles from a home ethereal
Are we, but dwellers on a wide, strange world
We have un-heavened with our disregard.
Ah! long have we the sweetness of her breast
Out-sucked with thankless lips, and babbled at
Some far-off star whose name we never knew,
And called her midwife who our mother was.

    *   *   *   *   *

To-day there are no gods; and men to-day
No longer sing like children-choristers

An unknown credo, clear and musical ;
And though there was a god, he passed away ;
The brow all thought august lies garlandless,
And only some remembered word or speech
Remains to mark the adoration gone.
A million idle altars still remain,
And still a million men grow pale in prayers.
Their lips have never yet unlearned to say,
Although the heart grew mute long years ago.
The spires of many temples still on earth
Yearn heavenward to-day in irony,
Like useless vanes that always face the south
When north winds winter the autumnal lands.
All gods have grown antique along with Jove
And all the shadows of forgotten gods,
And now the great heart of the old-grown earth
Beats muffled with a new and strange despair,
And grey-eyed Sorrow walks to-day with men,
Lamenting with her silent, mournful eyes
The time that was, yet never from her lip
Breaks forth one worded lamentation low ;
The sadder for the silence in her heart,
Her mute mouth quivers with a wild despair.
And yet her dusky form goes not alone,
But on her footsteps faint, disconsolate,
Goes one with dawn-light gleaming on her brow,
A laurel woven in her golden hair ;
The silent smile of power half plays around
Her lips compressed with all unuttered things,
And from her countenance a light out-shone,
Like morning glimmering on a ruffled sea,
While in her star-like eyes, dispassionate,
Yet sweet as tranquil Spring's awakened smile,
The shadow of a dream still undivined
Perplexed the perfect brow's soliloquy :

Like one who strives to hear a far-off sound
Of fading music dying on the wind,
When only one stray, transient echo comes
To tantalize the silent listener.
Some call her Science, some Philosophy,
But all men know the magic of her smile
That righted once and still rights olden wrongs,
And touched with dawn full many an olden gloom ;
And she to deep-eyed Sorrow spoke with love :
" Lament no more along the ways of men,
For morning reddens in the dusky East,
While twilight lingers still within the West.
Yet gather if you must pain's aftermath.
There are no gods to-day.   We mourn them not ;
For in their old-time, far-off fastnesses
They pined secluded, while man climbed in pain
The height he stands upon, though still in pain,
Uncheered by any voice of any gods.
For tongue of god was never heard by man
Except when sounded by a woodland bird,
Or murmured by the wind or running stream,
Or in some sound of nature, fugitive,
Forever faint, incomprehensible.
Yet why misname the music of the world?
We never dream divine its sounds unmusical.
Gods are the shadowings of man ; think not
That man is but the shadow of the gods ;
For they are all dethroned –nay, not dethroned ;
They crouched within the midnight's murky lap
That crumbled with the first touch of clear light ;
But earth has had its visionary days ;
And thou wouldst never walk to-day with men
But that some found a solace in thy face,
And some have seen within thy clouded eyes
A beauty more than vintage-laughter knows.

But pain and sorrow spring from suffering,
And suffering must ever mean disease,
While in their footsteps always follows Death.
But man, the child no longer, slowly learns
That pain is naught but the reproving bruise
Upon wild feet that wander from right ways ;
And though a million years his feet have bled
He still must wander from the one soft way
And bruise his erring feet on unseen stones,
Although those ancient blood-stains mark the way.
And on the long and gradual incline
He only sees the ever upward slope
By looking back far down the winding road,
As sky-larks never know the height they reach,
Until they pause upon their upward flight
And find their old world withered far away.
To-day man soars, not blind, but busily ;
His eyes bent on the end, his feet feel not
The weary miles that mark the slow approach.

So man, the tireless harvester of truth,
Up-gathers golden sheaf on golden sheaf,
No longer satisfied with flowers alone ;
And seeing Spring and Summer great with signs
He feels the autumnal fulness of all things,
Knowing full well no dream was ever dreamed
That shadowed not undreamed realities."

Then Science led pale Sorrow far from men,
And lulled her troubled heart with ancient tales
And olden legends strange, and stories of
Mythology, religion's sunset name ;
Then tells of astral and immortal things,
How man in time shall conquer earth and sea,

But greater still, shall know his own strange soul,
And hold at last all yet unfathomed powers;
Till peace across the tranquil world shall steal
Sweet as the slumber in soft Summer's face,
And man, no longer haunted with unrest,
Shall feel the fulness of all life and love,
And fall asleep when life's long golden day
Doth die away like some sweet melody;
And holding in his heart his memories,
He enters the eternal dreaming-while;
As children after some long holiday
Among the meadows and the flowery streams,
Outwearied, fall asleep at eve's soft hour,
Still holding in their sleeping hands the flowers
They gathered in the golden afternoon.
And then young star-eyed Science turned away,
And went once more among the ways of men,
Where many an undone task awaited her.
And though her goal still gleamed far, far away,
She knew full well her feet must falter not
Until they trod each long-sought alien way;
But she, remembering what had been of old
Of her promethean mission, sorrowed not.

    *   *   *   *   *

And wearily we twilight watchers look
Along the future's far-off winding way;
And though from earth the midnight glooms are gone,
There still lurk many old illusive clouds
That dusk the golden glimmerings of the dawn;
But in the fulness of all time the earth
Shall grow forgetful of its ancient wrongs,
As birds remember not the long night glooms
In winging sunward through the hyaline.

A SONG IN AUTUMN.

Ah, Love! can the tree lure the summer bird
  Again to the boughs where it used to sing,
Where never a song in the autumn is heard,
  And never the gleam of a vagrant wing?

Ah, Love! can the lute lure the old-time touch
  To fingers forgetful of melody?
Can we who have loved for a time overmuch,
  Lure back the old love as it used to be?

No, Heart! there is nothing in me to love;
  But come as a bird to the wintry bough;
Come now as you came when the blue was above,
  And summer shone soft on your girlish brow.

Steal back to my arms in the autumn's grey;
  While I who have waited thy coming so long,
Awake with the life of a long-gone May,
  When wild through the land rang a spring-bird's song.

*　　　*　　　*　　　*　　　*

Can summer elude the autumnal touch?
  Can love once forlorn of its spring grow green?
Can we who were lovers of old overmuch,
  Re-learn what is lost and relume what has been?

SHE SEEMED A WILD BIRD CAGED ON EARTH.

She seemed a wild bird caged on earth,
　Who fretted in her prison bars,
　　A wild bird brought from heaven's blue
Still unforgetful of her birth ;
　And while she gazed out on the stars
　　She sighed to look where once she flew,
　　Until at last her wings broke through.

Now thro' the midnight gloom I gaze,
　And should my wistful eyes once see
A new star drift down heaven's ways,
　I know she looks once more on me,
　　And by the astral barrier waits
　　Until my angel ope the gates,
　　And earth no longer cages me.

ON READING FAUST.

For Marguerite, the wild love and the woe,
　And then the sweet, still grave—the woman's lot.
For Faust, the impotent remorse, the blow
　To sense, and the experience pain-bought.

YOUTH AND LOVE.

A laugh lurked in your pool-brown eyes,
  A peach-bloom shade was on your cheek,
And you were wanton as the skies,
  And I was merry as a Greek.

Your hair fell wild about your face,
  And where your loose corsage hung down
A sun-beam pierced that secret place,
  And flecked your girlish breast of brown.

A flush across your dark cheek spread
  At every sultry kiss you gave ;
And yet you shook your little head,
  Although your eyes were tender-grave.

And laughingly upon your hair
  I used to place a wreath of flowers ;
Ah! summer seemed without a care
  When we played lovers in old bowers.

But you have changed, I know not why ;
  The brown has faded from your cheek,
And laughter from your wistful eye
  No longer breaks whene'er you speak.

But calm and pensive is your gaze,
  And clouded has your sweet face grown,
And your light heart of younger days
  Seems strangely hardened to a stone.
        *   *   *   *   *
Not that, O Love ;--ah! never stone !
  I see it now your full heart breaks ;
It is the child a woman grown :
  But were those old days all mistakes ?

A REVERIE ON ERIE.

Along the far-off misty hills
    Faint gleam a few white sheep that stray
Among the dusky purple rills
    That melt long miles and miles away.

The swallows from the high cliffs' walls
    With tireless wings cleave overhead,
And on the darkling waves their calls
    Grow thin, remote, and now are dead.

And voices, unknown voices, rise
    From out the dreaming waves, but we
Can only humanly surmise
    Their old unworded mystery.

And thro' the dark memorial gloom
    The moon-beam and the star-gleam steal,
And faintly through our human doom
    An ancient star-like hope we feel.

To-night the waves are long and low,
    And we who float upon their breast,
Are maddened that we never know
    The secret of the water's rest.

WHEN MELODY AND SORROW MET.

When Melody and Sorrow met,
　It was the autumn weather;
And Sorrow's clouded eyes were wet,
　When they two came together.

The lip of Melody grew still,
　While thro' her tears smiled Sorrow;
And winter crept across the hill,
　And snows came on the morrow.

Then Sorrow cried, "Though spring be missed,
　May we not fare together?"
And Melody and Sorrow kissed
　Amid the snowy weather.

And then the lip, long idly mute,
　Of Melody grew troubled,
Till Sorrow touched his silent lute,
　And lilt and tune out-bubbled.

And love shone warm from Sorrow's eye,
　And flushed her cheek grown hollow;
Till snow and winter wander by,
　And spring came with the swallow.

THE PASSING OF APRIL.

Thou girl of many a golden tress,
   Pale April, with the troubled eyes,
Along earth's vales once musical,
   The echo of thy music dies.

And down a far-off flower-strewn path
   I see the glimmer of thy feet,
That now forsake thine old-time fields,
   Where thou and I were wont to meet.

And with thee go the dreams thy breath
   Wreathed round my face that followed thee
In all thy woodland ways and fields,
   When earth was wide for thee and me ;- -

When earth was wide for thee and me,
   And in thine eyes of troubled grey
The light was soft with tears unshed,
   And life was sweet some unknown way.

I long to follow after thee,
   As swallows follow on the spring ;
And yet I see thee pass away
   On thine eternal wandering ;

And I turn back to earth forlorn,
  Where once thy sweet feet lingered long,
Where once they wandered through the fields
  And all earth's birds broke into song.

And now May comes across the hills ;
  But April, April,—thou alone
Hast touched thy lips too tenderly
  Through smiles and tears upon mine own !

PROMPTINGS.

On this strange stage where men and women play,
  When they, who linger on their half-learned lines
To look before and after, go astray,
  An unseen Prompter from without reminds

The actors of their half-forgotten parts ;
  And then the faltering Comedy takes life,
Out-laughs the grave-eyed Tragedy, and starts
  Anew to act the drama's ranted strife.

THE MINSTREL.

She was a princess far above me,
  And I, who loved her all the while,
And madly strove to make her love me,
  Was scarcely worthy of her smile.

But wildly sang I in her gardens,
  At dawn and dusk, noonday and night,
Until at last her heart unhardens
  While listening at her window-height.

And from my passion's pure persistence
  She can no longer hold aloof;
She comes without a thought's resistance,
  And takes me 'neath her regal roof.

And while in youth I yearned to capture
  Some laurel for my minstrel brow,
The longing is displaced by rapture,—
  Her white arms are my halo now.

Yet while my princess dreams beside me,
  I strive to strike my harp anew;
But with her love no more denied me,
  My songs are strangely faint and few.

And to my youthful wild endeavor
  My thoughts turn from this songless peace;
But youth's old songs are gone forever,
  While youth's old yearnings never cease.

IN THE NIGHT.

Across the hills the twilight steals,
  And in the gloom the birds grow mute ;
O'er field and vale a low bell peals
  Above one robin's last faint flute.

The timeless stars gaze down once more,
  And in the west the last lights pale,
And shadows gloom the ocean-shore,
  Where voices in the darkness fail.

The midnight hush is on the deep
  With silence far too full for words,
And through the leaves the night-winds creep
  More lyric than a million birds.

Then sea and earth and ancient star
  Seem blended in one voice above,
And wafts to me from realms afar
  The music of a far-off love.

And I who yearn with old-time pain
  To see thy face, O unknown power ;
For thee must seek once more in vain,
  In sky and sea, or earth and flower.

But still this truth I strangely feel,-
  I see it in each soft star's birth :
Although the night thy form conceal,
  Thine arm is round the ancient earth.

INDIAN SUMMER.

The soft maid Summer, with her languid loins re-girt,
　From Earth, her love of old, withdraws her cling-
　　ing arms,
Yet lingering looks again, and olden days revert
　Her thoughts, and all the dread that love alone
　　alarms
Can scarce subdue the wanton wildness of her heart.
　She stays, and turns upon her ancient love her face;
Then soft her yielding arms steal round him ere
　　they part,
And all grows dim in dreaminess of one embrace.

REMORSE.

Red lips that dumbly quiver for his kiss,
　And now but fondly touch his grave-yard stone,--
Ah! lips he loved of old, remember this:
　He had not died, if he had only known.

THE ROCK AND THE ROSE.

The grim rock on the hillside rough
   For ages stood the sun and storm ;
But once upon its shoulders gruff
   The wild-rose twined in rapture warm ;

For one sweet summer twined and clung,
   Then fell away and left the rock
More barren where the dry vine swung,
   The sterner for the dead arms' lock.

And through the endless empty years
   The rock remained.—But tell me, Man,
Who loved and lost, yet shed no tears,
   How with the rock where roses ran ?

THE PASSING OF MAY.

A hush fell on the tawny-throated choir
    That carolled from a thousand tuneful bowers,
And all those ceaseless voices seemed to tire,
    As passing May went down among the flowers ; –

Went down among the flowers and passed away,
    And left the old melodious vales forlorn,
When skies were blue and birds sang all the day,
    And dew clung sweet around her feet at morn.

And falling blossoms showered her farewell ways,
    While from old earth the vernal tremor went ;
For far she strayed without one backward gaze
    To those sweet days in maiden dalliance spent.

And now now no bird-notes ring the whole day long,
    But only in the dusk and dawn-light grey
There floats across the fields a robin's song,
    Who flutes a wild farewell to passing May.

THE FUGITIVE.

By night, for twenty nights, he crept
   Across the silent midnight land,
And stole each dawn within the woods
   To pluck wild fruit with trembling hand.

At last he reached the little stream
   That wandered round his home of old,
Then on along its well-known bank
   'He went, wrapt in the midnight's fold ;

And up the well-remembered path,
   Until above the brook's dim bank
The great, dark house he saw once more ;
   Then deeper in the brush he shrank,

And crawled beside the garden wall,
   And reached the old familiar lawn ;
And stole beneath his ancient home,—
   Then trembled as he saw the dawn,

And back along the brook he crept,
   And blurr'd his foot-prints from the sand ;
And then by night, for twenty nights,
   He stole across the silent land.

THE HARBINGER.

The foot of Winter lingered on the earth,
  And Spring still tarried on her southern ways,
And never a timid bird found heart to sing
  Through all the silence of the sunless days.

But only now and then a muffled chirp
  Came from some lonely sparrow in the cold,
As evening settled on the songless earth,
  And twilight mists across the meadows rolled.

Then morning dawned, and from the silver east
  The sunlight flooded all the humid earth,
And clear and sweet across the uplands came
  The fervid note of the first robin's mirth ;

Across the fields and through the opal air,
  With reminiscent thrill of memoried springs,
The reckless song of the first robin came
  Wild with the promises he sunward flings.

He carols from a leafless maple spray,
  With summer bubbling from his ruddy throat ;
And dreaming of the south's forsaken skies,
  There lingers in his song a southern note ;

And they who feel the dim, mysterious power
  That brings the spring-time bud to summer leaf,
Now know full well the promise of his song
  That glamours all the gloom of winter's grief.

Oh, could I read the secret of thy hope,
  Small bird that carols in the tree-top bare!
Oh, that I once could feel the golden June,
  Beyond the darkness of a March despair!

And yet more mellow wilt thou never pipe,
  Although a million bird-throats thrill the air
Through all the dawn-light of a summer morn,
  And on through all the fuller noon-day's glare.

And with more rapture wilt thou never sing,
  Though all earth's flowery vales are full of cries,
And every lyric valley through the land
  Resound with summer's endless melodies.

And yet, flute-throated bird, a note forlorn,
  The shadow of a sadness, fills thy song ;
The lonely harbinger that never hears
  An answering call, remote, and faint, and long.

But still sing back the Spring, mad melodist,
  For song and golden Summer follow thee ;
For all the music of remembered Springs
  Dwells in thy fluted carol's melody.

A MAN AND A WOMAN.

BEFORE.

While thus I hold thee warm and white,
While thus we soul in soul unite,
And all thy hair, thy face, thy form,
I hold and have, —where is the storm

Can wreck our love?

AFTER.

What dost thou do in thy grave, O Heart?
And do the days linger?
Why should a God in his heaven start,
And stretch out his finger

To wreck our love?

SONG AND LIFE.

This throbbing bird-throat far flung forth
Delirious melodies long;
And all the bird's life being sung forth
Seemed centered and lost in the song.

This bird-throat ne'er uttered a cry;
His life was the song that another sang;
And his wings beat wild thro' the songless sky,
While the note of the groundling skyward rang.

PAULINE.

Sails on the blue sea came and went,—came and
    went;
  They passed and faded away in the sea-rim's
    haze,
While many a swallow roamed through the summer
    air,
  And the sea-cliffs greyed in the heat of the summer
    days.

Life seemed full with a gladness strange, and a
    stranger sorrow,
  And summer was sweet with dreams as the air
    with flowers;
While I and a child on the cliffs stood hand-in-
    hand,
  And looked on the sea as it slept through the sum-
    mer hours.

Then from the sea and the sky she turned her child-
    eyes brown;
  " Love me your whole life long!" the childish lips
    exclaimed;—
" Love me your whole life long;" and her child-eyes
    looked in mine,
  And deep from her childish heart the sea-born pas-
    sion flamed.

Fresh came the breeze from the sea, and the August
 sky was blue,
 And the child plucked a flower that grew in the
  withered grass ;
And I took the flower from her baby-hand and placed
 it in her hair,
 For I knew that her love from my life like the far-
  off sails would pass.

Ah, child!—Ah, childish love, that the world will
 wither away !
 Thy love will come and go as the passing sails on
  the blue,
For summer and love and life are all in the end as
 one,
 And the words were only a touch of the sea and
  the summer on you.

To-day, of the flower and the child and her youth's
 wild words,
 There remains but the flower, and again I dream
  by the sea ;
And the far sails come and go in the blue sea's summer haze,
 And a withered flower and a childish word is a
  token of life for me.

THE REPROACH OF THE GODDESS.

I, toiling up the Apollonian slope,
A moment paused upon my tortuous way
And scanned the gloomy summit from afar
That all my younger dreams and older hope
Had clothed with golden brilliance like a star;
But only midnight glooms and twilight grey
Dwelt round the higher paths I strove to climb,
And frenzied, turning to my silent guide,
The mild Pierian maid who led me on
Amid the darkness of the upper slopes, I cried:
"Oh! whither, hapless woman, have I gone?
Is this the shadow of the mount sublime?
Enough of mockery, and enough of pain!
For still the unknown summit stands aloof,
And I had rather tread my old-time earth again;
Your gods are dumb,—their silence is the proof."
My guide then turned her star-like tranquil eyes,
Still passionless, towards the deeper night
Wherein the Temple of the Summit lies,
And spake into mine ear:
                              'Tis more the fight
Than all the idle guerdons to be won;
It is the worship though thy gods be mute;
Turn thou thy shadowed face toward the sun,
For Art is not the goal, but the pursuit.

*　　*　　*　　*　　*

And I gazed back down Art's dædalian ways,
And saw where many a thousand feet had bled,
Then turned toward the far-off mountain haze,
And saw it tinged with morning's glimmering red.

PYGMALION AND GALATEA.

I.

Enthralled within the sculptured stone, she sleeps ;
　But one long kiss the unknown barrier breaks,
And through the marble bosom warms and creeps
　The blood that tingles, till the woman wakes.

II.

And looking in your eyes of summer blue,
　No miracle the ancient story seems ;
For was not I once wakened thus by you,
　When one kiss broke through life's old clouded
　　dreams ?

III.

Though we to-day smile at the legend old,
　And care not whether dream or truth the tale,
We two well know, when life or love grows cold,
　That old-time Greek's one touch that cannot fail.

SUMMER.

Summer looked out from her brazen tower,
    And the sun flashed deep from her golden hair;
And she gazed to the North through many an hour,
    As her mild eyes filled with a maid's despair.

For Autumn, her strong-armed lover of old,
    Had wandered for long from her lonely side,
And her young heart aged and her breast grew cold,
    As she looked o'er the fields and the woodlands wide.

And her eyes once soft with a tender blue,
    Were dimmed with the grey of her silent tears,
And her gold hair in from the tower she drew,
    And down from the wall fell the brazen spears.

But her sweet face turned to the South again,
    And her eyes in their wistful depths flashed blue,
As she looked on the sleeping fields of grain
    And the fruit of the earth as it sun-flushed grew.

And the golden fields and the dreaming wheat
    Lay long in the arms of Summer in sleep,
And the heat of her lip on their cheek grew sweet,
    As the grain swayed down with her soft breath's
        sweep.

But the strong-armed wooer comes over the hills,
    And the maiden of dreams is drawn to his side;
And Summer shrinks close, and her warm heart fills,
    As they fare far down through the northlands wide.

TO A SINGER GROWN SILENT.

Song's wings too longingly had flown,
Until full wearily alone
They clove unwinged azurn ways;
Then glided down eve's golden rays,
And fluttered back to earth again;
Aweary of the wings' refrain,
Re-dreaming in their resting-time
The golden ways they once did climb.

Yet this, thy silence after song,
Can do thine exiled notes no wrong.
The sounds that soared from thee of old,
Wrapt in the wing they ne'er unfold,
Lie dreaming in thy clouded eyes.
And in thy bosom's fall and rise
Sleep more than song's mere memories.
On thy mute lips dwell melodies.

Wan Summer never smiled so sweet
As when she strayed with tarrying feet
Far down fair ways that southward wind,
And cast one lingering look behind;
Then earth's autumnal passion took
Its colouring from that one last look.
So when thy silent lips awake,
By being mute, they too will take

A sweetness from our yearning-while ;—
Like golden lands wide seas enisle.
But how can silence still make sweet
Thine harmonies of old complete ?
Touched with an art's too futile power,
No fairer blooms the perfect flower.

Yet why suspended each full note
That throbbed once from thy lyric throat ?
Was it that melody grew mute,
Enamoured of some silent lute
That harmonied with luring art
Within thy too melodious heart ?
Or was it that thy voice grew still
Because no striving might fulfill
Thy soul's great songs, grown infinite,
And startled with its own wild flight,
In knowing well the songs it heard
Could never fit to note or word ?
As dreamers lose themselves in dreams;
As we view not the sun's full beams
Till evening shadows softly shroud
Its strength in many a goldened cloud ;
A wing remembering not to fly,
In some wild flight's sweet ecstasy ;
A hand that cannot carve the form,
Because the sculptor's soul grew warm
With love for her who sat for him,
With too-alluring moon-beam limb.

When songs, no longer slumbering,
From thy full heart again take wing,
Be it when summer fills the earth
With many a tune of woodland mirth,
Lest we, un-heavened now so long,
Feel not the fullness of thy song;
Lest we become, re-paradised,
Discomfited by what we prized,
And heaven through the golden rift
Prove some too great, Tarpean gift.

THE ANARCHIST.

From out her golden palace, Fortune thrust
  A maddened dog, whose mouth foamed white with
      hate;
And loud he howled, and gnawed the court-yard dust,
  And ground his teeth upon the iron gate.

LOST AT SEA.

IN JUNE.

Beside the sea they stood, upon the cliffs,
  And swallows roved above the sun-lit waves,
And twittered round the fleet of little skiffs
  That rocked upon the slow sea's swells and caves.

The man, a brown-faced toiler of the sea,
  And she the girl who wedded him that day;
And both looked forth and thought eternity
  Could never rend that June-time joy away.

And through the long still summer afternoon
  They lingered looking out across the sea;
And twilight stole around them all too soon,
  And shadows fell upon their reverie.

For he and she, as man and maid of old,
  Stood dreaming olden dreams forever new,
While sunset tinged the west with red and gold,
  And all the wandering swallows homeward flew.

In September

The summer wanes, and all along the shore,
  The fishers' wives look often to the west
For sight of home-returning sails once more,
  While woman-fears rise in each troubled breast.

The early twilights shroud the sea in mist,
  And on the land has fallen autumnal gloom ;
For the returning wanderers exist
  Few lingerings of a summer's old-time bloom.

And down beside the sea a sad wife stands
  With wistful eyes bent on the far-off verge,
And shades her brow with two small sun-browned
      hands,
  And gazes out till dusk creeps o'er the surge.

Or, as she dreams upon the sandy dunes,
  And sees the waves grow grey at even-tide,
Her lonely heart remembers old-time Junes
  When he and she once sat there side by side.

And long before the first faint beam of light
  Has flushed the east, she peers through vapors grey,
Half-hoping that sometime within the night
  The longed-for sail had stolen in the bay.

Across the waves, whose song she never learns,
  No glimmer of the well-known sail appears;
And pale with fear and splashed with spray, she turns
  Away her face, all wet with bitter tears.

And strangely sad are those long autumn days,
  For spring seems lost beyond the long-gone years,
And life grows dark a thousand unknown ways,
  But still the lost sail never homeward veers.

The swallows flutter through the misty air,
  And gather by the sea for southern flight;
Not loath to leave for summer lands, they fare
  Away far southward through the silent night.

Like child-eyes gazing on some parting sail,
  That see the faint ship fade beyond the blue,
Her sad, dark eyes watch thro' the twilight pale
  The wandering birds before they southward flew;

Half longing that their wings might bear her far
  Beyond all sunset isles, beyond the sea,
Far out beyond the last land's harbour bar
  To where she dreams that one loved face to be.

THE RETURN.

At last the dreaming Indian Summer came,
  And sunlight smiled across the sea once more,
Until it grew and shone a golden flame,
  But summer's voices swelled not from the shore.

And when one tranquil morning tinged the sea,
  Upon the slowly rolling swells there lay
The little fleet come home again, and free
  Outswung the weary sails upon the bay.

But no voice cheered one waiting woman's heart,
  And ere they told her of the missing sail,
They felt she knew, and saw the tremor start
  Across her lips, and all her face grow pale.

But she had somehow dreamed it all along,
  And as she sat alone upon the sand,
She listened to the old sea's mournful song,
  A dirge her heart could never understand.

OVER THE SEA.

Far in the golden west the fisher sailed,
  And o'er the ocean waves his grey boat fled ;
For all his June-time love for her had failed,
  And now 'twas better she should think him dead.

So through the golden summer eves he sailed
  Away from his old love, as sailors steal
From their old sea-worn wreck whose timbers failed,
  And fled that he alone the loss should feel.

Perhaps 'twas better that she never knew
  He lingered exiled in an alien land,
That those deep old-time eyes of summer blue
  Were clouded with a hate she could not understand.

And now he lingers on a far-off shore,
  And looks back o'er the sea to his old land,
To his old love, both lost for evermore ;
  And hears the ceaseless waves break on the sand.

WORLD-WORSHIP.

The gruff world turns its heedless face away
From where the patient street musicians play,
And strive and sweat to catch its careless ear;
Yet all the world leans close to overhear
The song of one who waits and sings alone
Beneath a woman's window, never thrown
Wide open, like two willing arms, to take
Him in at last for all his passion's sake ;—
The great world strains to overhear his song.
But he, who sang and sorrowed all along,
Gazed ever to that darkened window-square ;
But for the listening world—what did he care ?

CAPTIVITY OUTLIVED.

We life-long captives, careless of our chains have
    grown,
In chasing on each heavy link strange scrolls and signs,
And of some old-time freedom only idly dream.
Enamoured of our toil, how may the mural stone
Be said to cage, since no man feels the bar, nor pines
To wander 'neath the stars that through some crevice
    gleam ?

THE RETURN OF SONGS.

It happened in a simple way,
  Yet how it came I scarcely knew;
Only for many a voiceless day
  Both heart and lip more silent grew.

It came about when day was done;
  A yellow gleam broke from the west,
Where glowed a cloud above the sun,
  That goldened all the earth's wide breast.

Across the clover crept a breeze,
  Beyond the fields a river gleamed,
A wild-bird sang amid the trees;
  And I was not what I had dreamed,

But one with wind and stream and bird,
  Even as the clover at my feet;
And every silent heart-string stirred,
  And life seemed strange and full and sweet.

TO CANADIAN POETS.

Far sweeter rings the song of Spring's first bird
That braves the sombre northland ways and skies,
And sings with all the warmth of its lost south,
Before the land is full of lyric cries,
When summer's ardour aids delirious song.
So dearer sounds the voice of one who sings
With hope of happier days, whose soul is strong
With fervour of a summer day divined ;
And deeper strike his notes than those of one
Who softer flutes throughout a sunnier day ;
And nobler is his task, because he throws
A light o'er lands that hereto lightless lay.

ELUSION.

He clutched the maid Delight, and held her fast.
Her back-blown hair flew round him like a cloud ;
But lo ! when down his hungering glance he cast,
His wild arms only clasped her empty shroud.

ISOLATION.

This thought thrilled through my inmost soul,
  As looking from the west's faint light
I saw the dark waves shoreward roll:
  All men, though fleeting on one flight,

Alone come in the silent race,
  Alone lunge to the end unknown;
Then wander far out into space,
  All desolate and still alone.

And each man's soul is space en-isled;
  Forsaken as the last faint star
That pales far down strange regions wild,
  Long-strayed, and ages lost afar.

THE SICK MAN.

He drew too near the brink, and peered below;
  And mirrored in that face of pain and fear
We saw gaunt horrors and abysmal woe
  Ere he could shrink back from the grim gulf's leer.

PROTESTATIONS.

Silent the lip,
And the lute is still;
Of song to-night
We have had our fill.

Silent the heart,
And our love is fled;
The shadows fall,
And the day is dead.

O silent lip,
And O heart, why mute?
Could a touch awake
Thy love, as the lute?

Then take the touch,
And O Love, awake,
And hold me once more
For the old love's sake.

*   *   *   *   *

Still silent the lip,
And the heart is still.
Ah, then of a life
I have had my fill!

CANADA TO ENGLAND.

> " — —*Our lusty realm
> Still dangles from an island's apron-string.*"

Sang one of England in his island home :
  " Her veins are million, but her heart is one ; "
And looked from out his wave-bound homeland isle
  To us who dwell beyond its western sun.

'And we among the northland plains and lakes,
  We youthful dwellers on a younger land,
Turn eastward to the wide Atlantic waste,
  And feel the clasp of England's outstretched hand.

For we are they who wandered far from home,
  To swell the glory of an ancient name ;
Who journeyed seaward on an exile long,
  When fortune's twilight to our island came.

But every keel that cleaves the midway waste
  Binds with a silent thread our sea-cleft strands,
Till ocean dwindles and the sea-waste shrinks,
  And England mingles with an hundred lands.

And weaving silently all far-off shores
   A thousand singing wires stretch round the earth,
Or sleep still vocal in their ocean depths,
   Till all lands die to make one glorious birth.

So we remote compatriots reply,
   And feel the world-task only half begun :
"We are the girders of the ageing earth,
   Whose veins are million, but whose heart is one."

TO ENGLAND ONCE MORE.

Though England's noon-day sun at last may set,
   Though all your summer draw towards a close,
We make thee mistress of all nations yet ;
   Our maple leaf shall redden to your rose.

Canadian hills and long Canadian plains
   Shall deck thine autumn wreaths with younger flowers ;
And close beside thee Canada remains,
   Remembering thy liberty means ours.

www.ingramcontent.com/pod-product-compliance
Lightning Source LLC
Chambersburg PA
CBHW021548270326
41930CB00008B/1419